Develop Marine Leadership in 24 Hours

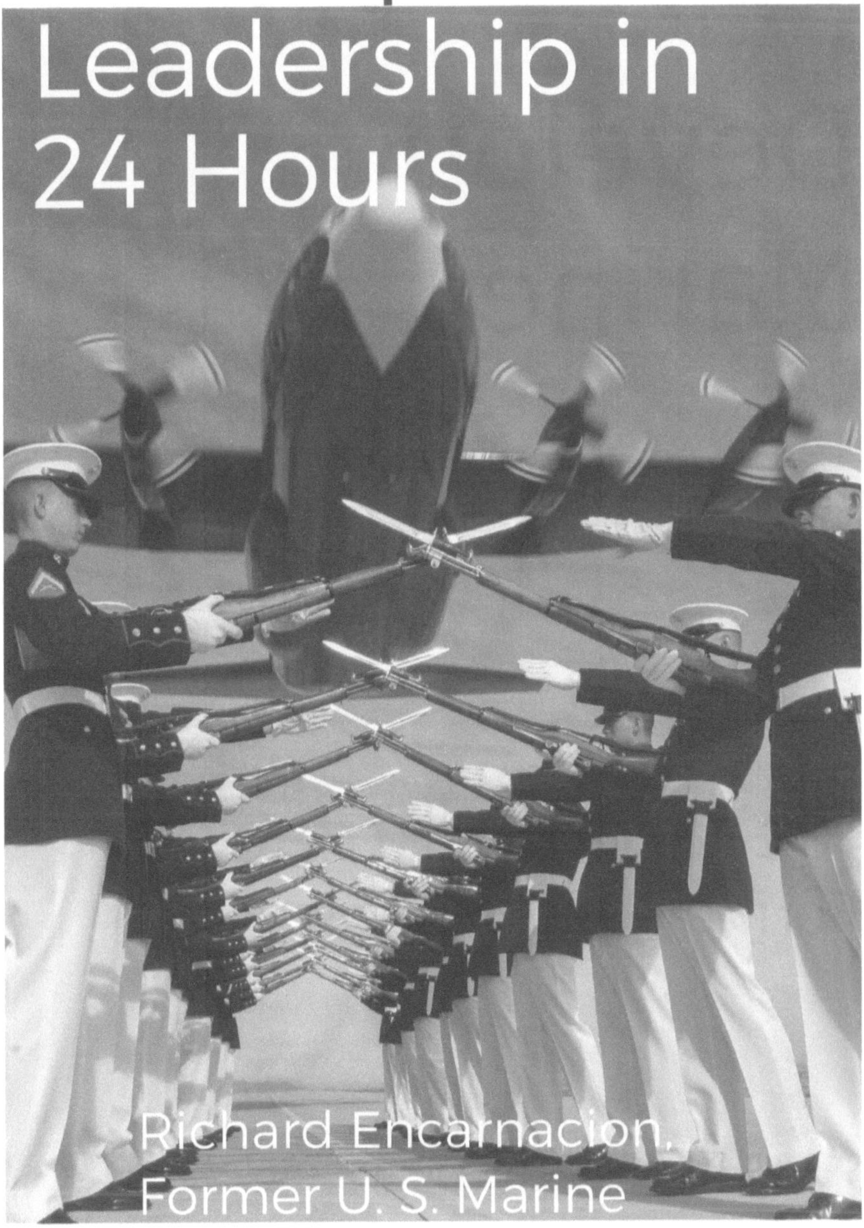

Richard Encarnacion,
Former U. S. Marine

Develop Marine Leadership in 24 Hours

Richard Encarnacion,
Former U.S. Marine.

Copyright © Richard Encarnacion, 2017.

All rights reserved. Without limiting the rights under copyright reserve above, no part of the publication may be reproduced, stored in or introduced into an archival system, transferred or transmitted in any form or by any means (electronic, mechanical, photocopying, recording, or otherwise) without the prior permission of both owner and publisher of this book.

This publication contains the opinions and ideas of its author. It is intended to provide informative material on the subjects addressed in the publication. It is sold with the understanding that the authors and publishers are not engaged in rendering medical, health, psychological, or any other kind of personal professional services. If the reader requires personal medical, health or other advice/assistance, a competent professional should be consulted.

The author and publishers specifically disclaim all responsibility, loss, or risk, personal or otherwise, that is incurred as a consequence, directly, of the use and application of any of the content of this book.

Copyright © Richard Encarnacion, 2017.

Table of Contents

Introduction

1. Leadership by design
2. Bootcamp
3. S.M.E.A.C
4. B.A.M.C.I.S
5. Semper Fi & Motto's
6. D.I
7. Managing vs Leading & Steve Jobs Syndrome
8. Perfect Uniform
9. Lead from the front
10. JJ Did Tie Buckle
11. What Is Your Leadership Style?
12. Blue Falcon
13. Five Ps
14. Billet vs Job
15. Fire Team
16. Be Ready In 24 Hour
17. The 4 B's
18. Take Charge of Your Post
19. Honor, Courage, and Commitment
20. Weakest Link
21. Quotes

Conclusion

"Be with a leader when he is right, stay with him when he is still right, but, leave him when he is wrong."

-Abraham Lincoln

Introduction

Marine Corps was born: Tun Tavern. November 10, 1775.

What is a leader? Someone who is a problem solver? a person who people trust? or someone who is a motivational speaker?

One of these or all these things, as a leader you need to be able to understand what motivates people. To make decisions, solve problems etc. Which will impact people's lives and the organizations, they belong to.

Here in this guide "Develop Marine Leadership in 24 Hours." You will learn to improve your leadership skills, from the level you're currently at. To grow into a higher level of leadership.

From the world's best leadership organization, the "United States Marine Corps".

You will get a glimpse within a few short pages, into the leadership lessons, words, beliefs, systems, idioms, and acronym. That Marines learn, about for leadership. And how you can apply this to your own personal life, business or society etc.

Richard Encarnacion, Marine

Chapter 1- Leadership by design

In this guide, my goal is to share some of the basic principles. That the Marine Corps taught me. When I first became a Marine, I know they are more than the ones listed in this guide.

But the goal, of this book, was not to list every single Marine Corp leadership principle. But to list leadership principles, values, and a thought process, from the Marine Corps. Which you can apply to solve your problems for leading people and understanding teams and leadership principles, so you can apply it to your situations.

Some of the Ideas, which I will represent are to be considered a starting point. If you were already a Marine. These might give you a reminder of things, you already learned. With ways, to incorporate it into civilian use, or corporate America. With the addition of some new concepts, and strategies to use them in non-military environments.

That is why this guide is written, specifically. For people, who want to learn more about Marine leadership. Who have never been in the Marine Corps, which can use this guide as a resource and read this information to develop some of the most effective leadership techniques in the world. Or learn to work with Marines. If Marine, apply the info to other tasks.

Either for personal or business use. Basically, translate the information and be able to apply it to other uses, rather than just military.

Develop Marine Leadership in 24 Hours

This small guide is to be used as a foundation guide, on the basic principles of leadership.

Which have helped, the Marine Corps considered the world's best leadership organization.

The two major goals, by finishing this material is for you to number one: Learn about Marine Leadership, principles and corporate applications.

The second for you to be able to apply this information.

Chapter 2- Bootcamp

U.S. Marine Corps, Bootcamp is three months long. The longest and hardest military training, out of all the branches of service in the United States. -DoD

Why do people become Marines? Not Sailors? Soldiers? Airmen? Coast Guard? **Who knows.**

The yellow footprints, when you first get off the bus in Paris Island or MCRD is the beginning of Marine Corps training and a transformational experience.

The cutting of your hair is a significant transformation. Where you are taught to earn, everything.

Why the Marine Corps?

Is it the uniform? Both men and women love the dress blues. Or Dress Black for officers.

The E.G.A, some like our insignia. The eagle, globe, and anchor.

Is it our motto: Semper Fi: "Always Faithful"

Our common word: "oo-rah..", which can virtually mean anything.

Being called: Devil or Devil Dog.

Or the feeling of being part of one of the best organization in world history? **Who knows.**

Even though, the Marine Corps is the smallest branch of the U.S. Armed Services. In Its history, our Marines have done extraordinary things.

The three months, of boot camp. Is imprinted on every Marine, as the day they stopped being a civilian and the day. They became a U.S. Marine.

It's a transformation, from someone who allowed the outside world to influence their decision making. To know working in a team based organization together to solve their problems, you can say is the best "leadership and follower organization in existence today.

There are many rules, but the basic principles of the Marine Corps. Are the same, whether you have served in "Vietnam", "Korea", "Afghanistan" or "Iraq".

Even the training stays consistent, everyone is "green".

Develop Marine Leadership in 24 Hours

Out of all the companies and experiences, I have had. The Marine Corps is probably the only organization. That regardless, of age, income, ethnicity, race or education you are considered the same as everybody else, and your achievements are based on your level of commitment, results, and drive.

Everyone for that reason is "green". If you are a male or female, you are simply called a "Marine".

Boot camp is simple. You have to give it everything you got, push yourself to your limit.

And when you are ready to quit, your Drill Instructors. Are going to push you beyond your limit, they gonna see your weaknesses and your strengths.

They are going to demand, more than you thought you are able to do. Either in the quarterdeck or in the sand pit, they are going to demand. You put out, what they want to see as a result. Not what you think you can do, they are going to demand excellence.

From Speed to get into formation with your squad, to precision doing rifle drills. To memory, learning life-saving steps, CPR, first aid and even Marine Corps knowledge.

And learning how to shoot a rifle, work on obstacles as a team. Finally, not be afraid to face problems head on.

Basically, to come out better than you went in.

Turn you from a weak body and mind to earning the title: U.S. Marine.

Richard Encarnacion, Marine

They not gonna give it to you, like in other boot camp training. You gonna have to earn it.

Chapter 3- S.M.E.A.C

The term "SMEAC" is a common term for Marines, in almost any job. As a young Private or even as a Sergeant Major, this word is used to get an understanding of what is going on.

This term can be utilized when trying to understand a complex situation. Which has hundreds of components, where there are people involved and there is a time limit or specific actions. Which have to be taken.

SMEAC can be used for situations. Where you want to break information down, from large amounts to smaller chunks.

S-Situation: Describe the reason for the task

M-Mission: Describe the task, time, place & Limitations!

E-Execution: Give the team the plan!

A-Ask: Ask if anyone has questions!

C-Check: Understanding of the plan.

How can you use this, in a different situation, setting or environment?

Example 1: If you are in a large data driven business, and have to work with engineers or data scientist. You can ask for the break down the big picture. Instead of reading 50-100 pages of information. This will give you a snapshot, of what is the plan. How it works and what is going to happen, how long it will take to complete and who are the stakeholders. Finally, if everyone understands their role. Basically, it saves time, money and energy.

Example 2: If you are in a fast paced business, sales or medical industry. And you have to make up-to-the-minute decisions about. Patients, Life and death situations, Purchasing, risk and rewards, using a word like. SMEAC will enable you to understand the capabilities and give you enough information to make a more informed decision quicker.

Chapter 4- B.A.M.C.I.S

Where S.M.E.A.C is an overview of the big picture plan, BAMCIS is an actionable term. Which is specifically used for leadership. In order to allow Marines or unit leaders to make decisions.

First, I am going to break down the term. Then I am going to talk about it.

BAMCIS, as is known in the Marine Corps. Is a Six (6) troop leading steps, from which the leader of the team receives the plans, and executes the mission.

These steps are logical and orderly in the process, for making the best use of time, facilities, and personnel in preparation for executing and completing the assigned mission.

1. **B**-Begin Planning

2. **A**-Arrange for Reconnaissance and Coordination

3. **M**-Make Reconnaissance

4. **C**-Complete plan

5. **I**-Issue Orders

6. **S**-Supervise

How can this term work, in a non-military capacity or occupation?

The beginning part of BAMCIS, the planning. This phase of the process is not just for a military team. But also for a firefighter team, police station or an emergency organization or situations, that are competitive or aggressive.

And can be utilized and adapted to understand, what steps to take to complete the mission. Or apply for working on complex projects, or business settings.

The first part, begin the planning. In this phase, you can do some "preliminary research", of what you might know let's say, about another business. If you're trying to compete with them or learn about the market for a particular product or service.

The second, arrange for reconnaissance and coordination. After you have your initial plan, you have to back it up with a plan. Either gathering intelligence by doing real life research, learning more about your competitor. "Getting the Right strategy to gather information."

To understand what your competitors are doing, and what you can learn or use to improve your current plan for your mission, company or project. The second part of that is the coordination.

Using the information gathered, to improve the competitive situation, between either corporations or projects.

Examples:
a. Price point
b. Service offered

To: "Observe and improve"

What the other organizations have, against your current organization, project or product.

And what you can do to beat them, compete or compare what you are doing.

Third, Make reconnaissance. In this part, are getting the intelligence and data, you planned out the business or the marketing plan. And you collected data at the different organization, which you compete with. And now you are ready to target the "weakness or strengths".

To improve the service offerings, you have versus similar services in the industry.

Fourth, you "execute on the plan" you utilize, the information and the real data to solve the problem. Both for the team and for your organization.

Fifth, you will be expected to issue orders to the right person, meaning either delegating to the right person. Or making sure that you have the right person for the right job.

Example: if you need legal advice, consulting with an attorney.

It would be counter-intuitive, to use a friend or family member for legal advice. Unless they are attorneys, their opinion would be nice. But it wouldn't solve the underlying problem, of having an expert legal solution.

Sixth, Supervise. Being able to have an understanding of the team and the people on the team.
And giving each member of the team a task. Which they will be able to complete.

This means, understanding each person on the team strengths and weaknesses and being able to count on each person to complete a portion of the task.

If you are not too familiar with the team, I would recommend. You spend at least one or two weeks, accessing your teammate's strengths and weaknesses.

Richard Encarnacion, Marine

Chapter 5- Motto To Live By

"Semper Fidelis- Always Faithful"

One of the reason, that I believe the U.S. Marine Corps. Is basically, a leadership operated organization is for a few reasons, but more than just the rank structure. Because the rank structure is not leadership, that is just your pay grade. Or time served, and promotions were given.

One of the values that Marines believe in, is that every Marine has the ability to lead. In the enlisted ranks from Private to Sergeant Major. We heavily rely on each member of our teams, to be responsible and dependable to accomplish the overall mission.

That is why we believe in small unit leadership, and as we will discuss in later chapter "fire teams". Thus due to this, the Marine Corps and its teams can accomplish more logistically challenging missions, which other military branches, are not easily able to do.

One of the Marine Corps, Motto. That I always remember from my days in the U.S. Marine is "We are as strong, as our weakest link".

Why is this important? I think, that many organizations. Outside of the military. Think that most Marines or military members are only able to do the very robotic task, and not think independently or be able to solve complex problems outside of the scope of their jobs.

This is false. Marines can do a complex task, involving leadership. Independent thinking and problem-solving.

As a former member of the military, I understand that our (MOS) or Military Occupation Specialty is not all we can accomplish.

The simplest way, I can explain this is. When you see a Marine Who is, for example, an administrator. Or a Marine who was some kind of technical (MOS) like air traffic controller, you can see that Marines are able to function outside the scope of just military work.

Because of corporations lack of understanding of service men & women capabilities. Many organizations are not finding the best capable people.

The same issues could be said for service members that leave the military with an infantry (MOS).

The difficulty in translating the skills of that occupation into something, which can be utilized in the corporate or business world.

And that is why I compiled a few sayings, or motto's utilized in the Marine Corps. Which correspond, to the entire philosophy of how many Marines think of teamwork and leadership.

And some of these sayings, have a direct application into the civilian workforce or to the corporate world.

1. **No Marine is Left Behind:** This mantra highlights the loyalty, teamwork, and brotherhood. Which exist among Marines.

2. **Improve, Adapt, and Overcome:** This motto conveys the resourcefulness, flexibility, and quick decision-making skills required to serve in the Marine Corps.
3. **Pain is weakness leaving the body:** Achieving more than your personal limitations dictate.

I mentioned these, to show the reliance and the determination of Marines to do the job.

Chapter 6- D.I. (Drill Instructor)

Who are D.I's? They are drill instructors, basically the military version of a trainer or job coaches.

Which help non-military members enter the armed services and train civilians, into active duty capable Marines. In other service branches, they have different names. But in the U.S. Marine Corps, they are called DI's.

Due to the short nature of this e-book, I won't discuss a lot of information about the drill instructor and recruit experience.

But the "boot camp" and drill instructor experience, is one that every Marine remembers. From the moment, they enter, either Paris Island in South Carolina or MCRD in San Diego.

Drill Instructors are the first introduction into the Marine Corps experience.

They are the first Marines, which a new recruit, becomes introduced to besides the "recruiter".

And their expectations, of what they will achieve with every Marine. They come into contact with.

Their motivation, and goal. Is to make every recruit to give up, and take away every possible weakness that they might have.

Push them, influence them. To withstand the distractions of the outside world, this is how the drill instructors mold, the new recruits. Into highly capable devil dogs.

In a period of three months, drill instructors mold clay shape bodies out of recruits, into a strong minded and fit fighting warriors.

The drill instructor basically grooms future Marines. In every possible way, from how a Marine should wear their uniform. How Confident a Marine should be, what are the values and belief systems that the Marine Corps uses?

And Hundreds of Micro lessons, and other examples. That this tiny book can never be able to capture.

Richard Encarnacion, Marine

Chapter 7- Managing VS Leading

Management versus leadership, what is the difference?

Organizations, when they have a business issue or the inability to solve a problem successfully. They are usually experiencing a lack of leadership.

How do I know this? Steve Jobs Syndrome. What is that? In John Maxwell Book, the <u>five-level</u> leader. Or in 21 leadership, traits. It talks about how to influence, impacts organizations and people.

In Steve Jobs case, as the founder of the apple. He was removed from the company he had started. After he took the company to success, due to disagreements with the board of directors of his company.

After Steve Jobs left Apple Inc. The company went down the drain, to the point to where it almost went out of business.

It wasn't to the point, where the company was almost out of business. That Steve Jobs, and was able to save the company.

But why? Some of the Marine Corps, Principles. That Marine Know, but that don't use after leaving the service. Which one?

1. Have a strong Opinions- Most people know in day are scare to talk about their opinions, and how that influences the organization.

2. Openness hurts sometimes- Steve Jobs was know for being brutally honest, like one of the Marine Corps Corp values.

Marines: Never Lie, Cheat or Steel.

3. Focus, focus, and focus. According to Walter Isaacson. Steve Jobs, Had an intense level of focus. Which you can almost say is obsession or just laser focus, which you often see associated with Marines. Due to the nature of our jobs being life and death, and being vital that we do the job right the first time.

4. Working in teams, jobs loved working in teams and loved meetings but hated power points. He felt that meetings should be about passing information. (Kind of like Marine Corps, Pass down). And how we love working in teams, if any branch knows how to work in team. Is the United States Marine Corps.

That is why, companies try to solve the problem. But they are not able to achieve the goal they want to compete or move the company forward.

Because they usually looking to find a manager, not a leader. That people want to rally around, and work with.

Many organizations, that need to solve these problems look "internally" first for a manager and then "externally."

The problem and solution are actually simple and yet complex.

Richard Encarnacion, Marine

Let's first look at the differences between a "Manager and a Leader."

Manager
Policies and procedures
Counting value
Power and control
Have subordinates
Managing work
Work Focused
Authoritarian Style

Leaders
Vision & strategy
Creating value
Influence & Inspiration
Have followers
Leading people
People focused

7 Things Leaders do, that Managers Fear

Leader
Connect daily goal with great work
think of people as people
want to earn respect
thrilled of teams achievement
empowers people
cares mainly about results
understand team shortfalls

Managers
Focuses on Short-term
sees the title or organizational charts
wants to be liked

is threatened
parcels out information as it cost him
is more concern with process
blames team

Management Styles

Autocratic: Retain Control, tells what to do, no consultation, subordinates to obey instructions

Impact: Helps complete urgent task, lack of creativity.

Paternalistic: Likes to take decision responsibility and caring attitude.

Impact: Helps complete urgent task, lead to a lack of resistance if employees have no input.

Democratic: Encourages participation, shares information, provides an opportunity for decision making.

Impact: Gains team commitment, particular when changes need to be made. Makes slower decision but employees usually support it.

Laissez-faire: Little to no direction from manager, subordinates are free to make a decision.

Impact: useful for skilled, trained teams, may lead to chaos without central control. Regular feedback and communication are required to work.

Leadership Styles

Commanding: Demands immediate compliance, "Do what I tell you". Drive to achieve, initiative, self-control.

When style works best: In a crisis, to kick start a turnaround, or with problem employees.

Visionary: Mobilizes people toward a vision. "Come with me". Self-confidence, empathy, change catalyst.

When style works best: When changes require a new vision, or when a clear direction is needed.

Affirmative: Creates harmony and builds emotional bonds. "People come first." Empathy, building relationships, communication.

When the style Works best: To heal rifts in a team or to motivate people during stressful circumstances.

Democratic: Forges consensus through participation. "What do you think?"

Collaboration, team leadership, communication.

When the style works best: To build buy-in or consensus or to get input from valuable employees.

Pacesetting: Set high standards for performance. "Do as I do, now". Conscientiousness, drive to achieve, initiative.

When the style works best: To get quick results from a highly motivated and competent team.

Coaching: Develops people for the future. "Try this". Develop others, empathy, self-awareness.

When the style works best: To help an employee improve the performance or develop long-term strengths.

The goal is not to use every leadership style available but to try to find out, what type works best for you.

But the goal is to use the leadership style, that works best with your strengths and the type of organization you work in and based on the goals that you want to accomplish.

Since this e-book is about Marine Corps development and leadership, many people think that the only leadership style utilized in the Marine Corps is **Autocratic**.

Although, that is one of the most common leadership styles used.

To accomplish a critical mission or goal, that is not the only leadership style in used.

You might ask yourself, how can a military organization with a rank structure, based on hierarchy use different forms of leadership?

It's really simple actually, it depends on the mission.

Richard Encarnacion, Marine

And what the job is that you are accomplishing on a daily basis, the more challenging position, which involves people with high-level skills. You see Marine Leaders utilize different leadership principles, such as democratic or paternalistic.

And some of the best Marine Officers, Enlisted NCO's and organizational corporate managers and entrepreneurs. Have a leadership style, that not only works with their personality but also is effective to run the organization.

Although, rank leadership is the lowest form of leadership. It is the baseline for the development of further levels of leadership skills.

The 5 Types of Leadership Levels: by John Maxwell

1. **Lowest Form of Leadership:** Title or rank- People follow you because they have to, not because they want to.
2. **Permission**- Relationship leadership, people follow you because they want to.
3. **Production**-People follow you because of what you have done for the organization.
4. **People Development**-People follow you because of what you have done for them.
5. **Pinnacle**-Respect, people follow you because who you are and what you represent.

Chapter 8- Perfect Uniform

More than any other distinguishable feature, which differentiates Marines, from Sailors, soldiers, and coast guard is the uniform.

Why is this important? Or why do Marines take so much pride in their uniform? And the indistinguishable "dress blues" or "dress black" uniform.

The distinguishable features, of difference between Marine Corps Utility, digis to deltas or dress blues. The Marine Corps uniform, not only provides a concealment and a level of respect for the service. But also a fashionable differentiation.

This is the reason, that Marines take pristine care for their clothing. One so they look their absolute best, when they put on their uniform.

Which is a presentation of who that individual Marine is and how much they care, but also following the regulations of the armed forces.

And quite frankly, because we are the best. So the better each Marine looks the better reflection into the entire "Marine Corps". And it's members, look good by association syndrome.

Chapter 9- Lead From The Front

Leading from the front is a sort of common word or thought process, which most Marines assume or expect from people, who are in a leadership position.

For over 241 years, Marines have been leading from the front in battles and wars. And also while at home, displaying a good example for both other Marines and civilians.

What this means to me, is that we are the first people in the engagement and as good leaders.

As Marines, we try to demonstrate leadership. By being first either in action in a firefight, or combat situation. Or first, to resolve a problem, why is this a good example for leaders.

In my personal opinion, leading from the front not only shows subordinates. That you are a leader capable of solving problems, but you also face challenges head on.

Because you have the courage to be the first, in the fight, aka situation.

The only situation where this could actually cause some issue. Is when as the leader, you are not the person who can immediately solve the pressing issue.

In this case, actually delegating the responsibilities, to someone on your team. Who has the direct expertise, is the best solution.

Chapter 10- J.J D.I.D T.I.E B.U.C.K.L.E

JJ DID TIE BUCKLE, is not only one of the most famous acronym in the Marine Corps. But it's actually the 14 leadership trait's which Marines, use to showcase their leadership.

It's also a *"Ditty"*, that is sometimes used when Marines are in boot camp. Ditty, meaning rhyme used to help Marines learn about the history.

The acronym. Represents a word, and each word. Displays leadership principles, which most Marines try to strive for.

J-Justice
J-Judgement

D-Dependability
I-Integrity
D-Decisiveness

T-Tact
I-Initiative
E-Enthusiasm

B-Bearing
U-Unselfishness
C-Courage
K-Knowledge
L-Loyalty
E-Endurance

Since the Acronym is mostly basic vocabulary words, there is no need for me to give the definition for them. When understanding, the meaning of each word.

But these 14 principles are the tenants of the Marine Corps, leadership.

Understanding them, and trying to implement them into your own personal life. Is the most important aspect, don't be intimidated. If you think you have to memorize all these words. And try to apply them into your life. I would recommend, you just use the words that most apply to your personal or professional life.

Chapter 11- What's Your Leadership Style

Do you know your current leadership style? Or what style, you can use that work best with your intended goal or your personality?

One of the best ways to identify this is to ask someone you know. What they believe your leadership style is.

Even though, you might assume. What your leadership style is. You might find out that your leadership style, might be completely different than what you think it is.

Feel free to go back, to the early chapter and see the different leadership styles and how they work best.

Although, they could be more than these four main leadership Types. For the purpose of this e-book, we are just going to focus on these.

The Four Main Leadership Types

Supporting: High Supportive and Low Directive behavior.

Coaching: High Directive and High Supportive behavior.

Delegating: Low Supportive and Low Directive Behavior

Directing: High Directive and Low supportive Behavior.

Also, consider the type of organization that you belong to and how will the leadership style and the duties of your position influence the behavior and actions of those under your supervision.

In addition to your understanding, your leadership style, and the organization you belong to. Being able to have a psychological perspective of how people behaviors work, in relationships to being put into a team is also important.

That is why, I wanted to introduce these principles.

Team Development Principles:

Forming: Team acquaints and establishes ground rules. Formalities are preserved and members are treated as strangers. (Hardest Part to overcome).

Storming: Members start to communicate their feelings but still view themselves as individuals rather than part of the team. They resist control by group leaders and show hostility. (Team begin to communicate).

Norming: People feel part of the team and realize that they can achieve work if they accept other viewpoints. (Finding similarities in each other)

Performing: The team works in an open and trusting atmosphere where flexibility is the key and hierarchy is a little importance. (Working together to solve problems).

Adjourning: The team conducts an assessment of the year and implements a plan for transitioning roles and recognizing members' contributions. (Working together without much supervision, because of team work and higher level efficiency).

Chapter 12- BLUE FALCON

The term blue falcon is a term mutually exclusive to the military. Which means, don't be a trader or lose the team trust.

Why do we speak about this? And why Is this important, when speaking about leadership?

The meaning of blue falcon represents not working against team cohesion. Not throwing people under the bus, which is to have people's back.

Even if blaming, your fellow colleagues would make you look better. The aspect of "blue falcon" someone, would have that person lose respect for you.

And if you wanted to work with them, in the future. You will not be able too because your reputation will be compromised with your co-workers and underlings.

I don't think there is anything further, that I have to explain.

Basically, don't take people trust for granted.

Chapter 13- Five Ps

The Five P's are more of a personal lesson from a former Chief Warrant Officer Aka Hammer Head, than a specific Marine Corps lesson. (RIP sir).

Even though, this lesson. Was from a Marine Corps Officer who was in the Marine Corps. His personal philosophy influenced my life, years after I had left the United States Marine Corps.

The Five Ps, represent the underlying reason why, some people are successful in completing task regardless of problems, obstacles or situations that present themselves.

Five Ps:
P-Prior
P-Planning
P-Prevents
P-Poor
P-Performance

(This is a nice way, to say it). Marine Corps, Six Ps.

Six Ps:
P-Prior
P-Planning
P-Prevents
P-Piss

P-Poor
P-Performance

Chapter 14- Billet Vs Job

What is the purpose of a billet? Or the difference between a billet and a job?

Billet: A position of a higher level of responsibility, beyond the scope of your regular job duties.

With this you have demonstrated higher level of skills, beyond the scope of just being a regular Marine.

Job: Your regular occupation, based on your (MOS).

In the Marine Corps, the level of leadership or judgment of trust. Which they feel you are capable of is in direct proportion correlated to the "billet" which you are tasked with.

Not necessarily your day job, you can have a basic job requirement and be tasked with a much higher level of responsibilities, if you have the leadership ability.

Chapter 15- Fire Team

A fire team, or a small unit leadership. In the Marine Corps, everyone has to be ready to lead. And this is why ranks, at lower levels. Have responsibility earlier, than in other branches of the armed services.

We train every Marine to lead, this is a great practice and habit. Because it teaches Marines to learn early. And take on more responsibility sooner, rather than later.

Speaking of fire teams, or small unit leaderships.

The breakdown is the following: How I translated it to Civilian Use from Military.

1. **Ready**- Riflemen **(Expert at Job)**
2. **Team**- Team Leader **(Leader/Manager)**
3. **Fire**- M249 **(General Expertise)**
4. **Assist**- Riflemen **(Support)**

This is the basic formation of a "fire team". Although, you might look at this and wonder.

What would be the purpose of this formation or team? And again, like in previous chapters. You might be asking yourself.

How is this information applicable? Or useful for business or a project?

Let's take a few moment's, and break this down.

The first, Ready. This is for the person or the riflemen. Who is spearheading the team, this doesn't mean he is the leader. But this is the person who is in front of the formation. **(An expert, Medical expert. A engineer, an account, a lawyer etc).**

For example:

The ready, let's say you work in a software organization. The "ready" meaning an individual could be a web developer or a software engineer.

Or any other person with a job, which you can see the skill set and ability of the person.

For this example, is someone who needs to be able to program, or has the expertise in a technology company.

The team, meaning the "team Leader". In the example above, the team.

Was the second, person in the formation. Why?

Because although, you do want to lead from the front. You also want to make sure, that you have the best person for the job upfront, and the leader to coordinate, between the team members.

In the 2nd position, obviously, these things are interchangeable.

I am just giving a basic formation example, which can be adjusted based on your needs.

Third, "fire" this is someone who has a vast amount of knowledge.

Maybe they are almost as good as the lead engineer.

But they have a more generalized knowledge, of different aspects of the technology business.

Thus, this is the reason why. They are the third member of the team.

And the fourth, "assist". Which is not for the least effective or most effective person, but someone who you can trust equally as any other member of the team.

But who would be more effective in an assisting role, rather than leading.

Richard Encarnacion, Marine

Chapter 16- Be Ready In 24 Hours

Be ready to deploy fast, as a former Marine I understand the 24-hour principle. Many people who don't come from a military perspective, might have a hard time understanding, why this is important.

Why is this important? When an emergency takes place anywhere in the world if the disaster or emergency is part of your mission. You want to be ready, within a short period of time usually 12-24 hours to take action.

Most people call this (QRF) or Quick Response Force. The most known are the "Rapid Deployment Force", which is part of the U.S. Marine Corps.

This places them in the category of "Forward Deployed".

Marine Expeditionary Unit, and other forces of the military. Use this 12-24 hour for mission readiness.

Why is this relevant to leadership? Or how can business leaders or manager use this in the business world?

The first reason this is relevant is that being able to respond to an emergency within 12-24 hours in any part of the world. Not only tells you, how prepared your Marines are.

But it also helps you understand your logistics and administration. Because you are able to make quick decisions to respond to immediate threats.

How can a business leader use this information, in a business capacity? One of the ways you can immediate take action on this is by evaluating your current team.

Not every organization will have a need to deploy to an emergency situation in the entire world in 12-24 hours.

But some organizations can have an emergency such as:

Example: Let's say you work in a truck company that transports beer, across different state lines. And three of your trucks have flipped over and two of your truck drivers are in critical condition in the hospital.

How can you apply the (QRF) to be able to solve this logistical issue?

For one, having a plan in place is good. But know that you have team members in harm's way, and merchandise that went out to stores is destroyed.

How to use (QRF) or a contingency to solve this problem, by having a 12-24 hour response plan.

You would already know if I lost all the beers. What truck can I re-route, that is the closes. To my deadline location, and where can I re-load with another truck even if the customer delivery is expected today. Let us say their two customers.

Richard Encarnacion, Marine

If both customers deliveries are expected at the same time, but one customer (merchandise). Has been destroyed, what can (QRF) do?

When you develop your contingency plan, you have a worse case scenario built in. And on this plan, you realize, that you have another truck closer to your location that hasn't been filled up with merchandise.

So instead of fulfilling the next order, you estimate. The time the truck that is on the road, has (ETA) estimated time of arrival to its destination versus the last truck (ETOD) estimated time of delivery.

And you realize that the truck you have in your location once is completely filled up with beer. Your truck will arrive there 15 minutes late versus the current one hour early.

So what you do? you coordinate with the truck driver and with the owners and managers of the facility and the customers of which you are making delivery and you explain the situation to them. And you let them know, that their shipment will arrive today as scheduled but around 15 minutes after the estimated previous time.

Will the customer be upset? Yes and no. Yes because you will be 15 minutes late.

Will the customer complain, no? Because you called him, explained the situation and you are still delivering the same day. What would happen if you didn't do this?

The customer which you had a logistical issue with the truck, would arrive one or two days late.

In addition, they would understand that there was an accident but. They would assume that you are not well prepared for situations such as this.

What will your customer think, if regardless of accident or emergency you was able to deliver the products?

I am assuming since I am not the customer, but if I was the business owner. I would trust the trucking organization with any order because I know that no matter the situation.

The delivery will come in, even if there is a situation that is not preventable.

I would see that this organization, is ready not only for truck deliveries but maybe even for bigger orders.

Chapter 17- The 4'Bs

These four, B's are the basic administration and logistics, information for handling troop welfare and dealing with enemy or prisoner of war situations.

In a non-combat related environment or in a combat related environment.

For companies or business leaders, taking a look at the four B's can have a big impact. Because you can quickly see, what you are focusing on in your team or organization.

And what you should be focusing on, basically. The most important things you should be doing versus what you actually are doing.

Beans- Rations, or troop welfare.

Bullets- Having the right Equipment

Band-Aids- Countermeasures if people get injured.

Bad Guys- Can be competition.

Beans- *Looking out for Employee welfare, honest wages benefits social functions, a good work-life balance.*
Bullets- *Having either up to date equipment or If can't have this, having better resources.*
Bandaids- *Providing your staff with either assistance or training to learn more.*
Bad Guy- *Learn more about the competitor. Your competition, another product etc.*

Chapter 18- Take Charge Of Your Post

The general orders are basically the rules every Marine must know by memory. Besides the riflemen creed, which Marines in their racks sound off at night, after a long day at MCRD or Paris Island.

They are eleven general orders for when Marines are on a post as sentries, and every Marine regardless of rank, (MOS) will be a Sentry or be on duty at one point in their career.

If you are a fellow Marine, reading this. This is not meant to bring out nightmares of boot camp, and sounding off on the top of your lungs to a drill instructor. And I will not even list the eleven general orders, I am simply going to talk about one general order, for the purpose of leadership.

Not always, but sometimes you need a base of guidelines. Which everyone can see, these are the basic tenets of the organization.

So for this reason, I am just going to talk about the first general order.

To take charge of this post and all government property in view.

As a Marine, this general order being one of the easiest to remember. But really, it makes a lot of sense. Because It's talking about when being on duty.

If you are in uniform and on duty, you should assume responsibility for all government property.

This is a little harder to translate into being utilized for other purposes.

For example:

If we are a security guard on watch, or a police officer or even a firefighter or some emergency service, provider. We should keep an eye, on government property and make sure that is handled correctly.

But in addition to this, the main reason that I think this has an applicable use. Is because, if you manage an equipment shop or a warehouse.

Which has millions of dollars worth of equipment, or valuable machine parts.

You want to take charge of your post, you want to ensure that you have everything categorized and logged. The basic principle, become more detailed.

Categorizing information, keeping track of inventory. This might seem mundane, but once something is missing or out of place your records. Will show either what happen or that you was responsible.

I have seen people in the business world, where this has happened to them and they been fired or arrested.

Taking charge of your job, and volunteering and doing more than asked too.

I will suggestion you use this example to determine your own applicable uses.

Chapter 19- Honor, Courage & Commitment

These are the Marine Corps Core Values you can apply something like this to your own organization.

This is basically, like a mission and vision statement.

To develop team cohesion, the Marine Corps is more like a Brotherhood. Then a traditional military branch.

Honor: Honor requires each Marine to exemplify the ultimate standard in ethical and moral conduct.

Courage: Simply stated, courage is honor in action.

Commitment: total dedication to Corps and Country.

Determining, what you care about. Not just this philosophy. But having a philosophy about life in general, working to solve complex problems.

Having set Smart goals, that are aligned with your personal philosophy. And what you believe about life.

S- Specific – Example:(I want to be a surgeon).
M- Measurable - Going to medical school.
A- Actionable - What are the steps.
R- Reachable - I have a 3.0 or 4.0 GPA.
T- Time bound - By the year 2023 etc.

This technique, will not only help you focus in. But become "Laser" focused.

Chapter 20- Weakest Link

"We are as strong, as our weakest link" -USMC

In the Marine Corps, one of the strongest axioms which I heard. Was we are as strong as our weakest link, I knew this had many meanings.

But one of the understandings that I had from it, was that we have to work together to offset each other's weakness. Some people might think of it as someone who is actually weaker, but I don't.

These sayings come to mind when trying to fight off or improve yourself. To become better than you are, because as leaders or someone who want to improve yourselves and become stronger humans, better people etc.

It is good to have something to kind of either guide or provide directions of how we will achieve a higher level of results or progress.

Marine Corps Leadership Principles

1.**Know yourself and seek improvement.** Evaluate yourself. By using leadership traits, and determine your strengths and weaknesses. Work on improving your weakness and utilize your strengths.

2.**Be technically and tactically proficient.** Before you can lead. You must be able to do the job, this is one of the problems in the corporate or business world. They promote someone they like, but not someone who has the skill sets first to do his job.

And be able to demonstrate your ability to accomplish the mission or project goals. And be capable of answering questions. Demonstrating competence in your job.

3. **Know your Marine and look out for their welfare.** Or know your team and look after then in a business, sense get to know them. What they struggle with, what they are good at, etc.

4. **Keep your Marines Informed**, or keep your staff your team informed. Keeping everyone on the same page, so they can see the plan. The goals and what each person responsibilities are.

5. **Set the example,** like we mentioned in previous chapters. Marines, we lead from the front. If you can't lead from the front because of not being the expert. At least set the example, of what you can do to make your team better.

How you deal with situations and solve problems. The same level, of commitment you show. Your team, they will show you.

6. **Ensure the task is understood, supervised and accomplished.** This can easily be applied to service or product organizations or even manufacturing because many times while working in corporations.

Managers make the mistake of assuming, that everyone understands the plan based on a chart. But we need to ensure as leaders, that we ask the team and see that they actually know how to do it. And are able to accomplish the goals, which are set.

7. **Train your Marines as a team.** Or train your staff as a team, train your co-worker.

8. **Make sound and timely decisions.** For emergency or time sensitive missions or plans.

9. **Develop a sense of responsibility among your subordinates.** Make people they care about what they are doing.

10. **Employ your command or business in accordance with its capabilities.** (Don't overreach, and stay consistent with your goals).

11. **Seek responsibility and take responsibility for your actions.** (Do what you say, say what you do).

Chapter 21- Quotes

I have just returned from visiting the Marines at the front, and there is not a finer fighting organization in the world! Gen. Douglas MacArthur, USA; Korea, 21 September 1950

Marines I see as two breeds, Rottweilers or Dobermans because Marines come in two varieties, big and mean, or skinny and mean. They're aggressive on the attack and tenacious on defense. They've got really short hair and they always go for the throat. RAdm. "Jay" R. Stark, USN; 10 November 1995

They told (us) to open up the Embassy, or "we'll blow you away." And then they looked up and saw the Marines on the roof with these really big guns, and they said in Somali, "Igaralli " which means "Excuse me, I didn't mean it, my mistake." Karen Aquilar, in the U.S. Embassy; Mogadishu, Somalia, 1991

Come on, you sons of bitches! Do you want to live forever? GySgt. Daniel J. "Dan" Daly, USMC; near Lucy-`le- Bocage as he led the 5th Marines' attack into Belleau Wood, 6 June 1918

Don't you forget that you're First Marines! Not all the communists in Hell can overrun you! Col. Lewis B. "Chesty" Puller, USMC; rallying his First Marine Regiment near Chosin Reservoir, Korea, December 1950

"Some people spend an entire lifetime wondering if they made a difference in the world. But, the Marines don't have that problem. Ronald Reagan, U.S. President; 1985"

Conclusion

This might be the end of this short e-book, but this is not the end of your growth as a leader. But I know that the information in this book will not just be nice reminder.

But it's something, which you can actually use an apply. Into different situation, I'm sure as heck. That you can use it when either leading a small team at a grocery store, a corporation or a big emergency response agency.

Use these tips, quotes, information, rules & philosophy. Do these principles work? Yes, as I am writing this page. Is the 241st year birth of the Marine Corps on November 10th 1775.

And all of these lessons, have worked in battlefields. In every part of the known "planet". Have been tested, and fought for with blood, sweat, and tears.

No other philosophy or guide in leadership can state, that their principles or philosophy have been used and has been proven for over two hundred years.

Today my friends, you join that elite group of people. Who know possess, the knowledge to become a better leader for your organization, yourself or for your industry.

Written by a former U.S. Marine, this is not just re-worded stories. This is real information, which I have used as former Marine. And in the business world, to achieve high-performance.

I know that many of you reading this. Might, have to re-read some of the information herein. To find how you can apply it to your life, situation or business.

By no means, does this book make you a Marine. You have to earn the title "U.S. Marine". But you have now learned, how different leadership works. And the different types of leadership styles, names and applications.

But Inside this guide, there is the hidden gem of the world's most respected military organization. For over 241 years, it has remained the world's #1 leadership based organization.

And thus if you apply some of the principles, and try to learn this idea you. My friend will also increase your leadership and you will develop a better understanding of how to lead people, in different situations and using different leadership styles.

**Author: Richard Encarnacion,
Former U. S. Marine**

Copyright © Richard Encarnacion, 2017.

www.ingramcontent.com/pod-product-compliance
Lightning Source LLC
Chambersburg PA
CBHW020712180526
45163CB00008B/3044